BREXIT: THE HEATH AND EEC CONSPIRACY

The Truth in Brief

The People's Brexit

Updated first edition July 2019

This book is dedicated to Nigel Farage, The Brexit Party, all Brexiteers and before them the Anti-Marketeers especially the Anti-Marketeer MPs who fought a valiant battle against Edward Heath and the EEC over UK membership of the EEC. Sadly for the UK and us all they lost this battle however the War still goes on and it is one that we WILL win and the UK WILL be a Democratic, Independent Country again free of the EU Dictatorship SOON.

Contents

Introduction

There has been political turmoil and Government lies and betrayal that led to the launching of The Brexit Party on 12th April 2019 by Nigel Farage and the success of the Party in the European Parliament Elections that resulted in the election of 29 fantastic, determined and committed MEPs that are going to change the current broken politics for good. This success will be followed by The Brexit Party contesting every by-election and potentially every seat in the House of Commons at the next General Election.

After this, it was felt necessary to publish an updated edition of this book. We also include a new chapter detailing our planned legal action against the Government and the EU regarding the Illegal, Undemocratic and Unconstitutional methods used to force the UK into the EEC/EU.

Anyone who is under the illusion that the UK entered the EEC/EU in a legal and democratic manner with the full approval of both Parliament and the People (as it should have done!) is in for a very rude awakening when you read this book! Corruption does not even begin to describe the whole EEC/EU experiment! This is the subject that is hidden by and NEVER spoken about by the Remain Establishment.

The People's Brexit are experts in research, Constitutional Law and political history and have been researching extensively on the subject of the legality of the UK being in the EU under both UK Law and International Law and we have concluded that the UK is in the EU Illegally, Unconstitutionally and Undemocratically for many reasons one of the main reasons being due to not getting the People's Vote, Consent and Mandate prior to entering the European Economic Community (EEC, the old name of the current EU) which it needed under UK Constitutional Law, this was necessary as it involved the surrendering of Sovereignty as well as major Constitutional issues, both of which were to a previously unprecedented extent.

It amounted to the UK being literally forced into the EEC against the will of the majority of the People. There were also many major Illegal abuses of power by both Conservative and Labour Governments between 1961 and 1972. In addition there were Illegal abuses of power by the EEC against both International and UK Law and against the Principles of the Treaty of Rome 1957 (the foundation of the EEC). Since then of course there has been further EU integration by means of stealth the Maastricht Treaty to name but one of the many Treaties further eroding the UK's rights and democracy. Democracy has also been abused, as Referendums on further integration have been denied to the UK People who were lied to by politicians and told 'it will not affect you, nothing will change' when in reality massive changes were made that affected daily life for everyone in the UK.

This all amounted to a conspiracy between successive UK Governments and the EEC back in the 1960s, 1970s and until the present day. This book exposes the facts and the truth that none of the UK Governments, the Establishment and the EU want the People to know even in 2019. This is this truth and history that has been covered up by the Establishment that want the People to only focus on today's situation and mess, not the reasons why the UK ever got in the EU mess in the first place.

It is the People of the UK that are having literally to pay the price for these illegal actions of their past politicians and the EEC/EU, as we have been paying for nearly the past 50 years. Crucially the UK's freedom, democracy and future have been stolen for these past 50 years and we can only dream about what could have been achieved if the People had been listened to, we would certainly not be in the nightmare situation of today as we would never have joined the EEC/EU!

Further the democracy of the UK was violated in order to tie it to a political body that was even openly acknowledged at the time of joining as being undemocratic with the vain hope that the UK could make it more democratic literally at the expense of the People of the UK and the sacrifice of our democracy! This has failed at enormous financial cost to the UK keeping it going all these years and what thanks is currently being given by the EU? Our 'friends' in the EU are anything but with the Brexit terms they have dictated!

One of the most tragic facts is that the UK was forced into the EEC by a majority of just 17 votes. That was the margin of 13th (a very unlucky day!) July 1972 when the third reading of The European Communities Act 1972 (the Act of Parliament that brought EEC/EU law into UK law) receiving 17 more votes for than the votes against, meant that the Bill had passed through the House of Commons. It was then forced through the House of Lords by the majority of biased and corrupt Lords and gained Royal Assent. All without a Public or Parliamentary Mandate!

Another tragic fact is that it was well recognised and the Heath Government even admitted to it, that the facts/ lies that they based joining the EEC on were nothing more than pure speculation and a 'gamble'. As a result of this 'gamble' the UK has paid many billions of pounds to the EEC/EU and is now going through purgatory, that could all have been avoided if the politicians had done their jobs and represented the will of the People and had just never embarked upon even negotiating to join the EEC in the first place.

Further, the People suffered greatly financially too, as before joining the EEC they enjoyed very cheap food as a result of efficient farming systems, Government subsidies and cheap imports from the Commonwealth. This was still the case before EEC membership, despite Heath putting up prices from 1970 (this was referred to in Parliamentary debate) to try to disguise future EEC caused prices rises and to get people used to paying more for food. Commonwealth Countries suffered greatly too when their trade with the UK ceased, causing great financial and emotional pain.

In reality there was no justification at all for the UK to join the EEC for reasons of trade or the economy or for any possible benefits and the reasons we did join were entirely political and wrong in every way.

Our Research

We have been able to extensively research Hansard (the official Parliamentary record of all debates and written questions for both the House of Commons and Lords) as never before possible, due to it now being freely available on the internet and what would have taken years, if it was possible at all, has taken months and is still ongoing. It has also been possible to assemble it in such a way as never before and compare it with other sources.

We were shocked and saddened by our findings of how the People of the UK were treated with such contempt by the majority of their elected politicians acting in self-interest and contempt of their Constituents instead of representing the People, to say nothing of the Illegal, Unconstitutional and Undemocratic practices used.

Many of the debates were not even witnessed by any of the press or public at the time, as they were late at night or very early in the morning and of course the press or public would not have seen the numerous written questions unless they waded through numerous volumes of Hansard.

We have uploaded some of this information from Hansard and other sources on our website (www.thepeoplesbrexit.org) for your information and will continue to expand on this but it is just the mere tip of the iceberg, such is the sheer volume involved. Nothing has been changed or altered just merely highlighted for ease of reading.

Every document has the full reference so that anyone who cannot believe what they are reading can check it for themselves on the internet! This is under Historic Hansard, 20th Century, where everything is organised in year and date order. A Hansard reference officially and for the purpose of this book is referenced as HC Deb and then the date and reference in full, this refers to House of Commons Debate/ written question. HL Deb refers to House of Lords Debate/ written question.

HOW DID THE UK REALLY GET INTO THE EU?

The short answer to this question is by the Illegal, Unconstitutional and Undemocratic actions of the democratically elected Politicians of the UK and the Illegal, Unconstitutional and Undemocratic actions of the EEC between 1961 and 1972.

The Illegal, Unconstitutional and Undemocratic actions of the Democratically Elected Politicians of the UK

This was with a campaign over more than a decade of lies, deceit, manipulation, brainwashing, Government sponsored propaganda, business and media sponsored propaganda, illegal actions such as distributing a favourably edited version of a White Paper that had not received Parliamentary approval and using Civil Servants to do it.

Also, the repeated denial of the People's Democratic Right to a Referendum or General Election based on whether or NOT to join the EEC and ignoring all Public Opinion of up to 84% against joining the EEC.

All three main Political Parties of Conservative, Labour and Liberal were led in by obsessive Pro-Europe leaders and all dissenting back bench MPs were belittled and ignored. Edward Heath, as the Prime Minister who finally forced the UK into the EEC, ignored the fact that he did not have a Legal Mandate from the People to join the EEC and lied to, bribed, manipulated and coerced MPs to back him in Parliamentary Votes (notably on 28/10/71) to join the EEC by force in the manner of a corrupt Dictator.

These are just some of the actions and tactics used and in our ongoing research we are finding more and more shocking details of how our Nation and People were conned and duped and denied their Legal and Democratic Rights by their corrupt, obsessed, deceitful, manipulating, self-serving Politicians.

The parallels of the situation with the past Politicians in the 1960s and 1970s dictating, that we join the EEC/EU, and the situation today with our current Politicians dictating, that we stay in the EU, all against the will of the People, is frankly frightening. It is history repeating itself of 'The Politicians VERSUS The People' instead of how is should be in a democracy, 'The Politicians REPRESENTING the will of The People'.

The Illegal, Unconstitutional and Undemocratic Actions of the EEC

The EEC exploited their advantageous situation to the maximum, whilst knowing full well that the People of the UK by an overwhelming majority did not want to join under any circumstances and knowing that the People of the UK desperately wanted a Referendum but were being denied one by the UK Government.

They should have DEMANDED that the UK Government carried out a Referendum (which is a well-established continental practice of consulting the People and did happen in 1971/72 on this exact issue for the People of Norway, Ireland and Denmark, the other applicant countries at the time) as one of their many terms of entry. It should have been on the straight question of yes or no whether the People of the UK wanted to join the EEC.

We assert that in not demanding a UK Referendum upon entry the EEC acted in contravention of International Law, Unconstitutionally and Undemocratically to the point of the suppression of the Democratic rights of People of the UK.

They did not want to demand a Referendum as they were purely motivated by the money and World influence the UK would bring to the EEC and they knew that the People of the UK would overwhelmingly vote <u>AGAINST</u> joining. This is in direct collusion with the UK Government who denied a UK Referendum on entry for this exact same reason.

It was also necessary for each of the other applicant countries, Norway, Ireland and Denmark to have a substantial majority in their Parliament in favour of EEC membership and it would have not been possible to join on a majority of just 17 votes with their citizens violently opposed as happened with the UK. Heath's Government took advantage of the fact there was no Written Constitution in the UK and the EEC just stood back and let this abuse of democracy happen and allowed him to sign their Treaty.

They also knew full well this was against the Treaty of Rome 1957 where it states in the preamble that the aims are '....to preserve and strengthen peace and liberty, and calling upon the other peoples of Europe who share their ideal to join their efforts...' There was certainly no liberty evident on behalf of the EEC just as there was no evidence of the People of the UK sharing their ideal, in fact the opposite was true!

They also took further advantage as they demanded punishing entry terms such as extortive financial contributions, forcing capitulation terms for agriculture and fisheries, having to comply with copious legislation, rules and regulations, having to comply with free movement of labour, services and capital and taking away many of our rights such as free trade and the abandonment of the Commonwealth. All against the will of the People and without the People of the UK being allowed to have their say and a Democratic Vote!

The EEC let Edward Heath sign the Treaty of Rome in 1972 knowing full well he did NOT have the consent of the People of the UK to do so and by doing this let the UK join the EEC Illegally, Unconstitutionally and Undemocratically.

The EU should now admit this desecration of democracy and compensate and co-operate with the UK to achieve Brexit on UK/ WTO terms.

The Constitutional Position

The UK has what is known as an Unwritten Constitution unlike most other countries, notably the United States that has a Written Constitution. The law in the UK has developed over the centuries by Statue and Case Law to form the Unwritten Constitution. However, this created a loophole with Treaty Law (based on arrangements with other countries that mainly started to be used in the 20th Century) that the Governments in the 1960s and 1970s were able to illegally exploit by effectively bypassing the main legal system and ultimately forcing the UK into the EEC/EU.

However, this exploitation cannot alter the fact that, under the Constitutional Law of the United Kingdom, one Parliament cannot bind future Parliaments. The only time this could happen is if it had the full consent of the People and even then it is arguable whether future generations could be bound in this way.

Therefore, when the Government joined the EEC on 1/1/73 against the will of the People this was an Ultra Vires (a legal term meaning to exceed power) Act that was against the principle of the Rule of Law, the fundamental foundation of UK law that the law applies to both the People and the Government equally.

Also under Constitutional Law a Government must not exceed its Electoral Mandate by introducing major constitutional changes which have not been fore shadowed (explained) by its Election Manifesto. This happened on three occasions with both Conservative and Labour Governments with negotiations that led to failed attempts to join in 1963 and 1967 and the eventual Parliamentary vote to join (allegedly in principle) the EEC in 1971.

Further, joining the EEC was in breach of the Bill of Rights 1689, which is the very foundation of our Constitution and Democracy, as it represented both taxation without representation and taxation by a foreign power, amongst many other breaches. Also, the ultimate foundation in the Constitution, the Magna Carta, has also been breached.

Possibly the most serious of all of Heath's Constitutional crimes was, by deceiving the Queen into signing the Royal Assent to the European Communities Act 1972 and effectively signing away UK Sovereignty and breaching her Coronation vows to the People and the Coronation Oath Act 1688, Heath actually committed Treason.

Relentless Campaign to Join the EEC, Lying to and Hiding the Truth from the Public

From 1961 throughout the 1960s the Governments were relentless in their efforts to get the UK into the then EEC. They still persisted after being refused entry in 1963 (and again we have extensive evidence from Hansard to this end) time and again denying the Electorate their right of a Vote whether or not to join the EEC and knowledge of the true implications of entry. Also they were relentless in getting further and further integrated with European laws and associations all without reference to the Electorate (we have much evidence of this).

Further, decimalisation and metrication were also measures taken to integrate the UK further in preparation of joining the EEC and VAT, a tax demanded by the EEC was introduced. Also from 1961 the UK deliberately started running down the trade links with the Commonwealth, turning away from countries such as Australia, New Zealand, Canada and India that had been there fighting with the UK in two World Wars against the main aggressor, Germany, that the politicians were now wanting the UK to join up with in the EEC. Trade with the EEC upon joining in 1973 only amounted to 20% as opposed to 80% with the Commonwealth and the rest of the world and when negotiations commenced in 1961 it was more like 10-15%. From even just a pure trade point of view membership of the EEC was financial suicide for the UK!

Many of the Electorate that should have had a vote on whether or not to join the EEC are still alive today and they are our parents and grandparents (the young people at that time, that the Politicians claimed were in favour of joining!) and they were betrayed by their politicians who lied to them over the true implications of joining, also they were brainwashed by the continual promotion of the 'Common Market' as the answer to all problems. Further, the general public of this time had very little information of Parliamentary activities and politics most relying on what little information had been fed to the newspapers and the politicians at this time were generally unaccountable to their Electorate and were seen as 'the elite.'

From our extensive research of Hansard it is obvious that all MPs and Ministers from 1958 and before knew about the loss of Sovereignty and political implications of joining the six countries of the EEC and most were determined to do it anyway with just a few that disagreed. They even spoke about the need to keep this secret from the people!

Early Conservative Government Position Regarding the EEC

The Conservative Manifesto from 1959 that the Macmillan Government were elected on did not mention the EEC at all (neither did Labour's). The closest mention in the whole document was under 2. Trade Opportunities when it said referring to the European Free Trade Association (EFTA):

"We are about to join an economic association of seven European countries; our aim remains an industrial free market embracing all Western Europe".

Then within months of winning office the Macmillan Government relentlessly continued their secret (from the People) mission to join the political union of the EEC citing 'policy change' if they were challenged on the issue.

The scheming and plotting of the late 1950s and early 1960s to get the UK into the EEC has been largely forgotten as it failed in January 1963 when President de Gaulle refused to let the UK join. This was only after 18 months of negotiations by the Government to join which were not sanctioned by the People.

In fact joining was NEVER sanctioned by the People at any point at all at any stage of negotiations over the course of well over a decade! The scheming and plotting continued relentlessly from January 1963 after the veto and was carried on by the Labour Government.

First Failed Attempt by the Conservatives to Join the EEC

In 1961 when it was decided to commence negotiation to join the EEC the Government did not even have a Mandate from the People to even start negotiations and in 1967 and 1971 the mandate had been for negotiations only.

We have extensively researched Hansard and have proof that the Government and all MPs of the time knew that they were taking the UK into a political union right from the start and that monetary union was planned. It was never the merely trade 'Common Market' idea that was sold to the People for years and called the 'Common Market' to lull the People into a false sense of security making them believe it was only for trade. Whereas it has never been officially just a 'Common Market' instead it was always the European Economic Community that was set on a course of political and monetary union from the start.

They also knew that they were denying the British people their Constitutional rights but ignored that in pursuit of their own aim to join the then Common Market at literally any cost.

They also knew full well that they were giving away British Sovereignty and according to Constitutional Law they should have either called a General Election on the issue in 1961 on whether or not to start negotiations to join the Common Market or had a Referendum on this point. Failing this they should have done the same in 1962, as negotiations were taking place, on whether to join or not, before the failed application to join was made in January 1963.

The first reference in Hansard on this exact point was 1st June 1961 (HC Deb 01 June 1961 vol 641 cc414-7):

Mr. du Cann Is my right hon. Friend aware that public opinion continues to be anxious on this subject? Although the economic implications of a British entry into the Common Market are largely understood, the political implications are not, and many people think that this decision whether to go into the Common Market is the gravest which Britain has had to make since 1939? In those circumstances, does not my right hon. Friend think that before far-reaching political arrangements are made there ought be some clear expression of opinion by the electorate either at an election or through a referendum?

The Prime Minister Of course I would not deny what my hon. Friend says, but I have not at the moment anything to add to what has already been stated.

With these words the Prime Minister (Harold Macmillan) himself both admits the political implications of the EEC and that the electorate should ultimately make the decision on entry but denies the people their Constitutional rights over their Sovereignty as he knew public opinion was against it and he would lose either an Election or Referendum and would have to give up the idea of joining in either case.

We believe this date, 1 June 1961, is significant as it is the date that the Government could and should have given the people their Constitutional rights by calling a General Election or Referendum based on this issue alone.

Instead of this the Government rushed through negotiations with no consultation of the people bringing the UK to the point of entry in January 1963 which was only denied by President de Gaulle. Many attempts were made by MPs to call an Election or Referendum but all fell on deaf ears. We have much evidence of this from Hansard.

Labour Continues the Lies and Deceit

In 1964 the Labour manifesto that they were elected on stated in criticism of the previous Conservative Government;

'How little they were able to transfer their faith and enthusiasm to the new Commonwealth was shown when Harold Macmillan and Alec Douglas-Home both declared there was no future for Britain outside the Common Market and expressed themselves ready to accept terms of entry to the Common Market that would have excluded our Commonwealth partners, broken our special trade links with them, and forced us to treat them as third-class nations'.

'Though we shall seek to achieve closer links with our European neighbours, the Labour Party is convinced that the first responsibility of a British Government is still to the Commonwealth.'

This was proven to be a lie and Wilson's Government just went full steam ahead to carry on where the previous Government left off in the relentless quest to join the EEC! Worse still, his Government was elected by the British People on a promise to effectively NOT join! This is a blatant abuse of democracy and makes another statement in the 1964 Manifesto nothing more than a lie and a joke;

'Labour does not accept that democracy is a five-yearly visit to the polling booth that changes little but the men at the top. We are working for an active democracy, in which men and women as responsible citizens consciously assist in shaping the surroundings in which they live'.

They further stated:

'Only with a new Government, with a sense of national purpose, can we start to create a dynamic, just and go-ahead Britain with the strength to stand on her own feet and to play a proper part in world affairs. We believe that such a New Britain is what the British people want and what the world wants. It is a goal that lies well within our power to achieve.'

Also, most hypocritical of all;

'Labour has resolved to humanise the whole administration of the state and to set up the new office of Parliamentary Commissioner with the right and duty to investigate and expose any misuse of government power as it affects the citizen.'

The Continuation of the Lies and Deceit by Labour and the Second Failed Attempt to Join the EEC

In 1966 Labour called an election with the intention of increasing their majority, which was very narrow. Hidden away at the back of their Manifesto (at page 24 of 26) after all of their main policies, probably missed by 99% of the Electorate, was a small reference saying:

'Labour believes that Britain, in consultation with her E.F.T.A. partners, should be ready to enter the European Economic Community, provided essential British and Commonwealth interests are safeguarded'.

These few hidden words Harold Wilson and his Government used to his advantage upon winning the Election, with his increased majority, and falsely claimed that it was a Mandate to join the EEC. In fact he embarked upon his quest immediately after and started negotiations again.

After his previous criticisms of the Conservative approach he even went further in his desperation to join making threats involving military co-operation and devaluing the pound along with numerous even worse than the Conservative concessions!

This was despite Wilson's previous political position that 5 conditions in the UK's and Commonwealth's favour would have to satisfied before joining, these were all abandoned along with the previously demanded changes to the Treaty of Rome (the only changes that would be asked for were the ones necessary to admit a new Member Country).

The agreed entry terms represented both unjust and unfair (punishment) terms offered by the EEC and a total capitulation on behalf of Wilson and his Government by accepting these terms. Wilson had also paved the way for his intention of forcing through EEC membership by the Royal Assent Act 1967 and the convenient abolishment also in 1967 of the Treason Act of 1940.

This all came to nothing when President De Gaulle vetoed the attempt again in November 1967. This was a second attempt to give away the Sovereignty of the British People without a Referendum or General Election on the issue (despite many requests in Parliament for both of these options).

Illegal Abuse of Power by the Labour Government

A crucial issue was after this second Veto, the application to join the EEC was never withdrawn ignoring repeated calls in Parliament for this to happen and despite extensive Public Opinion against joining the EEC. Wilson admitted many times that it was 'still on the table' as he described it. However, the Law is clear on this and the application should have been withdrawn immediately after it failed.

Eventually after President De Gaulle left office Wilson and his Government were able to merely carry on years later where they had left off with the application which was an Ultra Vires abuse of power and fundamentally against the Rule of Law. This is also in addition to the fact that things had moved on in this time and the EEC had become even more resolute to federal and economic union.

On the subject of the De Gaulle Veto, it was either the recognition by someone who claimed to be a wise long term friend of the UK that the EEC was not a suitable organisation for the UK's needs and future, which was the official line given. Or more cynically it was an attempt to buy more time to get the financially punishing (for the UK) Common Agricultural Policy in place to the maximum benefit for France. From our extensive research we have concluded it was the latter.

Final negotiations were set for July 1970 and the Wilson Government were all set to attend them when Wilson decided to call a General Election that he fully expected to win. Mainly because he did not want a General Election in 1971 (the latest time he could have it) as he feared there may be a backlash against him in this year from the People due to the introduction of decimalisation.

At this point it must be stated that all three main Party Leaders at the Election of 18th June 1970 were determined to take the UK into the EEC and were the three Patrons of the British Council of the European Movement (source: Hansard HC Deb 17 December 1969 vol 793 cc359-60W) an organisation existing only to promote European integration. The Electorate therefore had no choice on whether or not they wanted to vote for a Pro-Europe Party which is both Unconstitutional and Undemocratic.

It is also the ultimate insult to Democracy and the Constitution for any Party to claim that their Manifesto in the 1970 General Election gave them the Public Mandate to join the EEC when there was no other choice open to the Electorate (i.e. no anti-EEC Party of the main three Political Parties). However, this is exactly what the Conservative Party did in 1971.

Both the Labour and Conservative Parties had their plans for negotiating with the EEC hidden at the back of their Manifestos. Further, Edward Heath, the leader of the Conservative Party, gave the false impression he had 'cooled' on the EEC issue both in this Manifesto and in his interviews at the time in his attempts to get elected. This is nothing more than blatantly lying to the Electorate in order to get into power.

Heath's Conservative Government Commencing the Third Attempt to Join the EEC

On the 18th June 1970 the Labour Party under Harold Wilson suffered a shock defeat and the Conservative Party under Edward Heath obtained power. Edward Heath was a fanatical Pro-European and had conducted the first EEC negotiations between 1961-1963, when he was the Lord Privy Seal, in this post he was able to negotiate unaccountable to a Government department and largely unnoticed by the public.

One of Heath's Conservative Government's very first actions was to take over the existing negotiations from the Labour Government and to merely take their seats at the table of the final negotiations with the EEC in July 1970 using the existing Labour application and capitulation terms from 1967. In fact, this is even arguably the same application from 1961-63 as we can find no evidence at all of this being withdrawn after the first veto of 1963.

This is an Ultra Vires abuse of power to the extreme and again against the Rule of Law to just take over from a different Administration, especially when it concerned a matter of such great National and Constitutional long term importance and with such far reaching and binding implications.

The Law is very clear that any negotiations should have been started from scratch using a new application based on relevant considerations and terms from 1970.

The Doctrine of Ultra Vires

It is important to understand the Doctrine of Ultra Vires in this situation, Ultra Vires is Latin for 'beyond the powers' and if an act requires lawful authority to carry it out and does not have that lawful authority it is considered Ultra Vires and is therefore null and void.

From our research we have established numerous acts that were Ultra Vires by the Heath Government between 1970 and 1974 and also numerous acts by previous Governments all with relation to the desperate attempts to join the EEC.

For the purposes of this book we will focus on two; firstly it was Ultra Vires to constantly deny the People a vote by General Election or Referendum on whether or not to join the EEC and technically this counts as multiple counts of Ultra Vires.

Secondly, Edward Heath committed the most serious Ultra Vires Act against the Law, Constitution and the Democracy of the UK since the Magna Carta was signed when he signed the Treaty of Accession to the EEC on 22nd January 1972 without the Mandate of either the People of the UK or Parliament.

The Capitulation Negotiations

It is important to highlight the competence of the 'Negotiators' between 1961-1971, they were deliberately not accountable to anyone, i.e. a Select Committee or Parliamentary Commission and would just report back on their 'progress' to the House of Commons.

It is Unconstitutional and Undemocratic in the extreme that the whole future of this Country was left in the hands of these inexperienced and unaccountable civil servants and Ministers. Much of the information reported to the House of Commons was classified as 'confidential' in the detail.

These negotiators were no match for the hardened EEC Negotiators and they took full advantage of that fact with their 'punishment' entry terms. European negotiators 'never give an inch', a fact that was noted by MPs as far back as 1958 (source: Hansard).

There were also many secret meetings of talks, negotiations and deals not even known to Parliament with Presidents and Prime Ministers of the six EEC Countries.

Further, in the negotiations they did not even ask for any special conditions as Ireland and Norway had in their negotiations. There were also further conditions they could have insisted upon based upon conditions obtained by the original six for their individual countries. Even worse, was the strict interpretation of terms that was opted for, in order to further shackle the People of the UK to the EEC.

In 1970-71 the most experienced EEC negotiator, Edward Heath, never even took part in the negotiations himself, giving more weight to the argument and comments made in Parliament at the time that these 'negotiations' were nothing more than a sham and everything was already all 'sewn up' on the basis of the capitulation Labour terms of 1967.

In fact in the view of many MPs the final terms were even worse than these having started from a position of extreme weakness and the EEC knowing that the Heath Government were 'desperate to join at any cost', to quote many an MP at the time.

It is also worthwhile to mention that the EEC founding six countries had taken several years prior to completing the Treaty of Rome of 1957 in which time they had put in many terms favourable to their own Countries (especially Germany and France). The UK had to just accept it in its entirety with no amendments other than the ones relating to the admission of a new Member Country. This is also unfair and undemocratic on the part of the EEC.

The EEC should have also insisted that as a term of entry that the UK Parliament did carry out a Referendum to ascertain that the Public did want to join the EEC and were not being taken into it against their will (as did happen!) as many other Countries had.

At the time that the UK was in the process of joining, the other EEC applicant countries Norway, Ireland and Denmark all had Referendums. Again, it is another example of the cold, calculating, self-serving ruthlessness of the EEC, who were only concerned with the financial advantage of UK membership and not about whether The People of the UK actually wanted it.

There was even the Legislation in place for a Referendum in 1971 that could have been used any time before joining, it having been brought by Tony Benn MP. Heath knew he would lose any Referendum held and would have to resign as Prime Minister and joining the EEC would then become impossible, so he did not permit it.

The financial contribution demanded by the EEC from the UK was unfair and exorbitant and increased substantially and rapidly over the years and as well as effectively paying millions of pounds to most of the other countries (with the rebates they received) it almost bankrupted the UK and is still a massive financial burden to this day.

Further, with the amount of emphasis currently placed upon the legal aspects of Brexit it is crucial to highlight the fact that the legal position of joining the EEC was entirely based upon an outdated White Paper produced by the Labour Government in 1967. Based upon this and the Illegal actions involved in joining it is ludicrous to claim that the UK is legally bound to the EU at all as the UK membership is null and void.

Devious and Illegal Practices by the Heath Government 1970-1971

In the General Election of 18th June 1970 the Electorate did not have a choice of an anti-Common Market Political Party as the leaders of the Conservative, Labour and Liberal Parties were obsessed with joining the EEC and indeed the three were the three Patrons of the British Council of the European Movement, where many other MPs and Lords also held leading roles (HC Deb 17 December 1969 vol 793 cc359-60W).

Indeed, successive Governments had been handing out large sums of money (up to £7,500, which was a lot of money then) hand over fist to many Pro-Europe Movements since 1962-63 (HC Deb 17 December 1969 vol 793 cc358-9W).

Also, according to a report in the Guardian in October 1971, over 2,000 European Legal Statutory Instruments per year were being integrated into UK Law with only a few being debated, and this was BEFORE joining the EEC! So the UK was already in the process of entering the EEC by stealth and had been since the 1950s.

The Little White Paper of Lies

The scant (a mere 48 pages including the covers) White Paper that was produced by the Government in July 1971 entitled 'The United Kingdom and the European Communities' (Cmnd 4715) for the benefit of Parliament and the People (in a censorious edited format on the rare occasions it was available to the People) consisted of numerous deliberate lies and omissions.

This was the basis for the decision to vote with the Government for many non-Conservative MPs on 28/10/71 and the official basis for the Government claiming it was in the best interests of the UK to join the EEC. Examples of these lies were at paragraph 29 'There is no question of any erosion of essential national Sovereignty' and at paragraph 31 'The English and Scottish legal systems will remain intact' and 'In certain cases however they would need to refer points of Community Law to the European Court of Justice.'

In fact the Legal, Constitutional and Sovereignty implications did not even warrant their own section under the contents and were just lumped under 'the political case' in paragraphs 26-39.

The biggest of the many omission was obviously since the day the Heath Government took over negotiations from the Labour Government in June 1970 they had accepted the fact the UK would have to take on the burden of Community Law (just the rules and regulations were over 2,500 in number and 42 volumes on their own not even counting the Treaties and mountain of thousands of pieces of secondary legislation!) and the fact that this Law would take direct effect and will be precedent over UK Law.

This document in itself is Ultra Vires (as amongst many other things it falsely claimed that it was the Government's decision to make to join the EEC), Illegal, Unconstitutional and Undemocratic.

This White Paper was so bad that even the Heath Government themselves favoured a White Paper produced by the Labour Government in May 1967 instead. However, this cannot mitigate the fact that this White Paper of lies, misleading and omissions is their official legal basis for entry to the EEC.

This is backed up in the debate of 20/1/72 when Mr Ronald King Murray commented in his speech "If one looks at the White Paper which the Government presented to Parliament in July 1971 on the central issue of the budgetary contribution of this country, one sees that the matter was dealt with in an extremely cursory way in paragraph 96. Great pressure had been brought on the Government to elucidate the financial obligation which Britain would permanently acquire as a result of signing the Treaty of Accession." He then went on to say that the answers received from the Government on this important point were evasive and meaningless.

It was also a fatal legal flaw in the application that no further White Papers were produced for the benefit of Parliament and the People between July 1971 and January 1972 when the Treaty was signed with regard to the final position on Fisheries and the Commonwealth and obviously the true implications of membership of the EEC and the Constitutional and Legal implications.

The Scandal of the Factsheets and the Short Version of the White Paper

When Heath announced in the summer of 1971 that the sham negotiations were over and it was the Government's intention to join the EEC he sanctioned a series of 11 'factsheets'. These were made available free of charge in Post Offices. It is thought that he did this so that the smallest number of People could see them as possible and 11 in number so that people could not see the true picture of what joining entailed unless you have all 11, and even then you are only seeing what the Government wanted you to see.

This is in direct contrast to the publication in the very same year, 1971, of 'Your Guide to Decimal Money' where "15 million copies of booklets were distributed to households before the postal strike" according to Mr Higgins (HC Deb 16 February 1971 vol 811 c1589).

There is no reason why all of the Government information (in one booklet as opposed to 11 factsheets) regarding joining the EEC could not have been sent to all UK homes in the same manner as the Decimal Money Guide, other than the reason being the Government was trying to hide the facts and deceive the People.

These factsheets were clearly very limited in availability (allegedly there were 10 million produced but that does not even equate to one million of each of the 11 factsheets for the entire UK!) and it has been asserted that the contents of them constituted an <u>Act of Treason</u> particularly with regard to the issue of Sovereignty and people at the time who did manage to see one complained bitterly to their MPs and the Leader of the House of Commons on this point, but all complaints were ignored by the Government. Also demands in Parliament for the production of a factsheet of the arguments AGAINST joining the EEC were denied.

These factsheets were only arguably available to housewives and pensioners. However, a Voter from 1971, who WAS a housewife in her 30s then, has recently confirmed to us she saw no such publications in her weekly visits to the Post Office or indeed even knew about these 'factsheets' until we informed her now!

There were also allegedly posters advertising them that no-one ever remembers seeing and a television advertisement promoting these factsheets that the Government confirmed in Parliament was made at a cost of £2,500 but was NEVER broadcast (HC Deb 03 August 1971 vol 822 cc295-6W).

Also five and a half million copies of a very favourably edited short version of the White Paper were printed and distributed by the Post Office in the same manner. This was a scandalously small amount and, at most, one third of the quantity required for each home to have a copy. Also, as it was being distributed through the Post Office instead of posted, very few people got to see it.

The total cost of producing all these publications was given as £647,550, including £191,000 for the short version of the White Paper. This was Taxpayer's/ Voter's money for something they never even got to see, let alone read!

This whole sham was brought up in Parliament when Mr John Mendelson stated (referring to the short version of the White Paper) "… I believe it is unlawful for the Government to have engaged in the distribution of a political propaganda pamphlet through Her Majesty's Post Office…" (HC Deb 27 July 1971 vol 822 cc510-29). This related to the fact that this White Paper had not been approved by Parliament and as such should not have been distributed at taxpayer's expense by the Civil Servants in the Post Office, this debate which took place at 7.39am on 27/7/71 (clearly unwitnessed by the press or the public) makes a very interesting read with the severity of the arguments raised and the clear misconduct of the Ministers involved.

Refusals of Select Committees and Royal Commissions

Heath and his Ministers (as with all other Governments wishing to join the EEC since 1961) also refused all the many demands for a Select Committee to be appointed to examine and report on potential entry and the terms involved, for example by Mr Arthur Lewis in March 1971 (HC Deb 24 March 1971 vol 814 c128W).

Similarly demands for a Royal Commission again by Mr Arthur Lewis, "to inquire into all matters connected with Great Britain's possible entry into the European Economic Community, the signing of the Treaty of Rome, the terms and conditions of entry, and to include on the Royal Commission, representatives from the Commonwealth countries of Australia, New Zealand, Canada, the Caribbean and one from the Channel Isles." This fair and democratic request for consultation and safeguards for the interests of the UK and the Commonwealth was rebuffed with an undemocratic "No" by the Minister (HC Deb 29 July 1971 vol 822 cc163-4W).

No research or studies were permitted at all between 1961 and 1972 by any Parliamentary Committees or any independent external groups or organisations to examine the facts of what membership of the EEC would entail for the UK and to determine any benefits that would be obtained and the disadvantages. Also to determine the true implications with regard to the Legal system, Constitution and Sovereignty. This is because the Politicians knew the truth would be exposed and that there were no benefits of membership to the UK only expense, loss and penalty. Also the terms agreed should have been made available for full scrutiny and further negotiation.

The whole situation was farcical, as no-one had the slightest idea whether there would actually be any benefits at all of joining the EEC. There should have been numerous studies done on the subject and it is very telling that one of the first things the Government did after the legislation was forced through, was to appoint several Select Committees on how to implement it.

By denying these basic and essential safeguards of further research and study into the implications of EEC Membership for the People of the UK and the Commonwealth, Heath's Government was acting as a Dictatorship and rightly this behaviour would not be permitted by a Government today.

The Ignoring of the People Regarding UK Entry to the EEC

The People were totally powerless regarding the entry to the EEC and their opinions were totally ignored and all calls for General Elections and Referendums on whether or not to join were denied. The People were an educated and sophisticated Electorate but were being treated with contempt by the politicians as would have been the case in the 17th and 18th centuries. From our research we can conclude that even the Victorians in the 19th century would have treated their Electorate better.

It is probably the biggest denial of democracy the UK has ever known which is all the more shocking that it happened in the 20th century not long after two World Wars had been fought against Germany which the UK was now being forced into the EEC with against the wishes of the People including Veterans of these wars.

The only real power the People after the General Election in 1970 had to express their disgust and opposition to Heath's Government betrayal of the UK and Commonwealth in joining the EEC against the will of the People of the UK was to elect an anti-Common Market MP at by-elections in a protest vote.

For example the Labour anti-Common Market candidate at Greenwich, Richard Marsh, was elected on 8/7/71 with a majority of over 70%. (HC Deb 08 July 1971 vol 820 cc1516-7). Unfortunately, he and the other anti-Common Market MPs elected with this protest vote, then just joined the back benches to be ignored like the will of the People by the Dictatorship Heath Government.

Another important factor is that there were also many social, economic and political issues that were distracting the public from potential entry to the EEC. The Vietnam War was going on, there were miners and other strikes, there were states of National Emergency due to power shortages and unemployment was extremely high. The main reason for the high unemployment was that Heath was hoarding money to make the balance of payments attractive for EEC entry and this had a serious knock on effect to the national finance and as a result employment.

So as a result, Heath's obsession with joining the EEC has ruined everybody's lives in the 1970s and to the present date.

EEC Joining Announcement is made by Heath

After announcing intended entry of the EEC deliberately and conveniently not long before the summer recess of 1971, there were some Parliamentary debates at the end of July. Heath also instructed all MPs to speak to their constituents and get their views. Requests from MPs for the provision of the short version of the White Paper or any other information for their constituents even in such modest quantities as 5,000 were denied.

All the 'views' obtained were obviously ignored by the Government as this was clearly just a 'fobbing off of the MPs' exercise to distract them from what was obviously 'a done deal'.

In the Conservative Manifesto for the General Election of 18th June 1970 Heath stated:

'Our sole commitment is to negotiate; no more, no less. As the negotiations proceed we will report regularly through Parliament to the country.'

This is the Mandate he used to take the UK into the EEC against the will of the People, one that he plainly states would only involve negotiation 'no more, no less'. This in itself is totally illegal and a betrayal of the People.

Heath's Lies to the Electorate

Further in May 1970 in the run up to the General Election Heath reaffirmed this by stating in an interview "It would not be in the interests of the Community that its enlargement should take place except with the full-hearted consent of the Parliaments and peoples of the new member countries…." Also on the BBC programme 'Election Forum' Heath stated around the same time "…no British Government could possibly take this country into the Common Market against the wish of the British People…"

Even worse that this was the fact that Heath further stated on the 'Panorama' television programme 'a week or two' before the Parliamentary Vote on 28/10/71 that it was still his view that "No British Government could possibly take…this country into the Common Market against the wish of the British people" (extracted from the speech of Harold Wilson, HC Deb 28 October 1971 vol 823 cc2076-217).

Wilson went on to state, referring to strong support Heath claimed to have to join the EEC "…The CBI no doubt, the Chambers of Commerce, the employers, the merchant banks – oh yes! But not the trade union movement not the pensioners, not the housewife, not even the Housewives'

54

League, if it exists today....The right hon. Gentleman holds his office not by the suffrage of the organisations. He has no mandate, for he sought none and obtained none, to take Britain into the Common Market except with the full-hearted consent of the British people. That is not at his command, and no vote of this House can of itself redeem his personal pledge to the British people.

We have warned what it must mean for the right hon. Gentleman, by whatever subterfuge, to take a divided and embittered people – divided and embittered by his policies – into Europe. Let him now seek from those people the mandate he spuriously claims by submitting this, and all his policies, to the free vote of a free British people."

The British People never got their free vote on whether or not to join the EEC. The final Vote was only in Parliament on 28/10/71 and in reality it was everything but free for the MPs.

The Vote is not secret and the Conservatives had 100 definite 'Payroll Votes' (i.e. Votes that would be rewarded by a Peerage, Knighthood, Ministerial role, keeping such role or even just keeping hold of a political career) and there were at least another 100 probable 'Payroll Votes'. Many MPs could not bring themselves to vote with the Government so abstained, many others had been brainwashed with the constant barrage of propaganda themselves or did not understand the true long-term implications of joining the EEC, and so voted with the Government. The Conservative Whip was also employed to arm-twist any of his MPs that dared to want to vote against the Government.

There was also a request made for the rules of the House to require Members to disclose personal pecuniary interests before this vote (suggesting external financial motivations were being given to MPs by businesses and individuals), unsurprisingly this request was dismissed by the Minister (HC Deb 07 July 1971 vol 820 cc420-2W).

Heath won by only 112 Votes in Parliament on 28/10/71 (there were 356 Ayes and 244 Noes) to join the EEC and no doubt all his Conservative Government Ministers and MPs got their 'pieces of silver' as reward for their 'Payroll Votes' at the sacrifice of the People of the UK!

The 87% of the people who predicted in an opinion poll 'we will go in anyway' despite what the People of the UK thought, were proven right!

Hiding the Truth about the EEC/EU and Deceiving the Public and Parliament

The Remain Voters and people who support the European Union have been systematically brainwashed and lied to into thinking it is a wonderful thing to be a part of and not realising the reality of it.

This is exactly the technique the Governments used in the 1960s and 1970s and to this date to get people to accept it and to agree with it and until only recently the People were not even given very much information about it other than what politicians wanted them to know!

The People of 1961-1972 were NOT given their say and worse than that were deceived, lied to, vital information was withheld and they were not told the true long term federal, political, legal, economic, trading, free movement and social implications and plans to this end of the EEC or even what adhering to the Treaty of Rome in its entirety REALLY involved, and we have much Hansard proof of this.

In fact there was a Parliamentary conspiracy to hide these facts dating back to 1957 and the birth of the Treaty of Rome. Also at the end of the day many of the MPs and Ministers did not understand the long term implications of all of these issues themselves and a lot of information was withheld from them by the Ministers involved!

A succession of both Conservative and Labour Prime Ministers acted like a Dictator in a Totalitarian Government between 1961 and 1972 denying the British People their say in their Sovereignty being given away to other Countries including one, Germany, who was previously the enemy around 20 years previously. Peace Settlements and military occupation were even still going on at this time as a consequence of this War!

As the political implications and loss of Sovereignty had been known from the start by all of the politicians of the day this represents a total betrayal of all the millions that died in this War and the millions that fought against this type of dictatorship and oppression that was clearly demonstrated by the British Governments back in the 1960s and 1970s.

The Secret Foreign Office Report on Sovereignty (FCO 30/1048)

The question of Sovereignty was analysed in an internal document of the Foreign and Commonwealth Office (FCO 30/1048) before the European Communities Act 1972 was passed but this was not available to the Public until January 2002 under the 30 Year Rule.

This document was only seen by Heath and a couple of his Ministers and should have been at the very least have been available to all elected MPs. If this had been the case there is no way that the UK would ever have joined the EEC.

Hidden away in this document under 'areas of policy' was stated 'Parliamentary freedom to legislate will be affected by entry into the European Communities' for customs duties, agriculture, free movement of labour, services and capital, transport and social security for migrant workers. The document concluded (paragraph 26) that this was acceptable and 'power' and 'influence' should be put before 'formal sovereignty'.

The ultimate betrayal was the shocking conclusion in this report that by the time, many years later, the People realised the deception, the UK would be too far integrated into the EEC/EU for anyone to do anything about it.

This document, now freely available on the internet, is proof that the Country and People were betrayed by Heath and joining the EEC represented the death of UK Sovereignty, Independence and Democracy.

Of course the EEC has since become the EU with even more of a stranglehold over the UK all without the People of the UK being able to have say on the matter. All as a result of the lies and deceit and manipulation of the People from 1961 to this day.

All of the information regarding the REAL implications of joining the EEC/ EU should have been made available from 1961 onwards to the whole UK not kept secret from the People and even using the 30 Year Rule to keep these secrets.

This is nothing but a conspiracy and a total abuse of Democracy.

The Referendum Issue

Referendums (along with General Elections on the Issue) were demanded on a constant basis from 1961 onwards to allow the People to be consulted on whether or not they wished the UK to join the EEC. They were always dismissed with a firm "no" or claims that it was not "normal practice" etc.

There was even an attempt to force a 'Common Market Referendum' under the Ten Minute Rule in 1969 (HC Deb 10 December 1969 vol 793 cc442-50) under the Wilson Administration based on the fact that Referendums had already been granted to the people of Gibraltar and the Falkland Islands amongst many other arguments in favour. This motion was of course denied and makes extremely interesting further reading.

A further desperate attempt under the Heath Administration to force a Referendum on the 'Common Market' based on the 'abhorrence' of the Government signing the Treaty of Rome even with 'the approval of Parliament' was attempted by Mr T.L. Iremonger (Ilford, North) under Motion 217 in January 1971 (HC Deb 20 January 1971 vol 809 cc1079-220). This Motion was abruptly refused by the Speaker.

Indeed, the facility was even already in place in 1971 for a National Referendum on joining the EEC that could have been held at any time before actually joining. This was down to a Bill, European Communities (Referendum) [Bill 170] that was presented by Tony Benn (first reading, HC Deb 14 May 1971 vol 817 c753) (second reading, HC Deb 21 May 1971 vol 817 c1759). This then could have been used to effect a Referendum at any time in the following over 18 months before the UK officially joined the EEC on 1/1/73.

Also the other EEC applicant countries of Norway, Denmark and Ireland were all having Referendums upon whether or not to join, this issue was brought up in Parliament in July 1971 and was as usual dismissed and suppressed by Heath (HC Deb 06 July 1971 vol 820 cc1123-4).

The People finally got their say at the 2016 Referendum (the sham Referendum of 1975 does not count!) and despite the lying and deceit that has carried on to this day the majority managed to see through it. So you can imagine if the true facts were known at the time and they had actually been given one, what the result of a 1961 Referendum would have been!

There is no doubt at all that the People of the UK were Illegally, Unconstitutionally and Undemocratically denied their legal and democratic right by successive Governments between 1961 and 1972 to have a Referendum on whether or not to join the EEC. Also in 1961 on whether or not to commence negotiations in the first place.

As a result of the Government's refusal to permit a Referendum on whether or not to join, the EEC should, in accordance with International Law and the principles of Democracy, have DEMANDED one as a term of entry.

It is also the ultimate in hypocrisy that Heath DID hold a Referendum, only not on EEC Membership, instead for the People of Northern Ireland over whether or not they wished to stay in the United Kingdom. This was because it suited him and he wished to break up the Union. This was yet another example of how he was not fit to be Prime Minister of the United Kingdom and was a disgrace to this high office.

Parliamentary Vote on Entry on 28/10/71

In 1971 there were 12 days of House of Commons debate, 6 in July 1971 before the summer Parliamentary recess and another 6 at the end of October 1971. This culminated in a 'vote in principle of joining the EEC' which was held on 28/10/71. A particularly devious aspect of this vote was that it was not just a vote in principle of joining the EEC, it was also a vote to accept the capitulation terms negotiated by Heath's Government, an argument that was later used many times to their advantage.

There were 600 votes cast, 356 Ayes, 244 Noes and many MPs abstained due to being unhappy about this Vote. If the MPs were truly representing their constituents with Public Opinion being over 70% against then it should have by rights been 600 Noes. As it was many MPs did say No and the final majority was just 112 Votes. Ultimately, that is what took us into the EEC and into the EU and the mess we are in today.

Much doubt can be put on the validity of the 356 Aye Votes. We have evidence of 100 definite 'Payroll' Conservative Votes and a further 100 probable 'Payroll' Conservative Votes that were alleged at the time. A 'Payroll Vote' is a Vote with the Government with the promise of a Peerage,

Knighthood, Ministerial Role, political favour, or even just to protect a political career or hold on to a Ministerial position. There was also evidence of 'arm twisting' by the Conservative Whip.

There was also the threat of the Government as a whole resigning leaving the Country in chaos. It would also force a General Election meaning that MPs jobs were literally on the line. Heath also knew that even if the whole Government did not resign he would have no choice other than to resign as Prime Minister if he lost this vote and as a former Chief Whip he was able to use his considerable talent to ensure he did not lose the vote.

There was also pressure on MPs from businesses hell bent on the UK joining the EEC so much so that the issue was raised in Parliament about whether MPs should declare their interests in advance of the Vote on 28/10/71 but this was dismissed. There was rife suggestion that some MPs had received financial and other incentives in return for their vote for joining the EEC.

A lot of the MPs including the non-Conservative MPs that did not stand to benefit from a 'Payroll' Vote had been systematically brainwashed and lied to into thinking the EEC was a wonderful thing to be a part of and not realising the reality of it. They themselves had fallen for the Government Propaganda and subsequently voted to join. They were also under the illusion that it was just like a club that you could just join or leave at will. Many also had an arrogant attitude that they should ignore their constituents and 'they knew better'.

Further, only around 30% of Conservative MPs had declared to their Constituents in their personal Election Manifestos in 1970 if they were for or against the EEC and for most MPs the EEC was not even an issue that was mentioned at all. Of course the issue of actually joining EEC had not even been regarded a possibility in 1970.

A lot of Labour MPs did Vote yes, led by Roy Jenkins, despite the official Party line being to Vote no and they were defying their party in doing so. At the Labour Party Conference in early October 1971 the members had voted over 5 million against joining the EEC compared with only 1 million in favour, this represented over 83% against joining and was the largest Referendum of the Electorate prior to joining. Wilson's attitude was to Vote against the Government based on the terms achieved not on the concept of joining that he still whole heartedly believed in.

An official Gallup Poll in July 1971 found that 87% believed "we shall go in any how" so that is conclusive and damning proof that the People were not fooled and believed that all Heath's lies, manipulation and misleading would mean joining the EEC against the will of the People.

There was even suggestion in Parliament in 1971 that it was suspicious that Heath could afford such things as a yacht. But the Charlemagne Prize for Services towards European Unification and the associated prize money said to around £75,000 or £1.5 million equivalent today (Source, 'Treason at Maastricht' by Rodney Atkinson and Norris McWhirter) that he received in 1963 would be have useful for this. It is also interesting that Roy Jenkins was also the recipient of this same prize and money in 1972 for his services in enlisting Labour MPs to defy the official Labour Party line against the Government and get them to vote to join the EEC.

In summary, this Vote was an outrage and an insult to the Constitution and Democracy of the UK by those who were democratically elected to serve the People.

Between the Vote of 28/10/71 and Commons Debate of 20/1/72

The non-binding Parliamentary vote of 28/10/71 was consistent with the usual perfectly planned timing of every element of the forced joining of the EEC. Our research of events since that manipulated vote exposed that the negotiated terms of fisheries policies were deliberately withheld from Parliament until the last possible opportunity of 13th/ 14th December 1971.

So poor were the terms given (amounting to a total capitulation) the Government knew it would severely impact on the vote of 28/10/71 were they to be revealed before the vote despite all their manipulation and even before the very last acceptable opportunity of the week before Christmas Parliamentary recess.

Similar tactics were also used for the final poor capitulation terms for New Zealand and the Commonwealth Sugar Agreements, both of these issues also being very contentious.

They were able to get away with this due to claiming that these three matters had not been concluded in the original negotiations and Parliament had no way of checking whether this was correct as most of these negotiations were conducted in secret and deemed 'confidential' and were not reported on by Ministers.

After they eventually discovered the truth, the Opposition were given a supply day (20/1/72) in order to debate these Fisheries terms. However, they were then forced to sacrifice the Fisheries Debate, after it was announced on 21/12/71 (the second last sitting day before the Christmas recess) that the Treaty of Accession to the EEC was going to be signed on 22/1/72 without prior debate and it was obviously necessary to use this supply day to at least have some form of debate on the Treaty at the expense of the Fisheries terms. This is a very good example of how calculating and corrupt the Heath Government actually was.

The Prime Minister also revealed in answer to a written question (HC Deb 20 January 1972 vol 829 cc251-2w) that he would be visiting Strasbourg on 21/1/72 in order to receive the European Prize for Statesmanship in the course of a session of the Consultative Assembly of the Council of Europe.

He went on to state that, whilst he was there he would be the guest of the foundation which had awarded him the prize.

This prize would have included a large cash sum, the amount of which we have been unable to establish, but it would probably be similar in amount to the £75,000 already awarded to him in 1963 for the Charlemagne prize (equivalent to £1.5 million today) it may even have been more allowing for inflation and the two cash prizes together would be worth over £3 million today, rather more than a few pieces of silver and paid to Heath for literally selling out the UK!

However, it has been a very good return for the EEC/EU with the multiple Billions we have paid them since!

House of Commons Debate on the European Economic Community (Treaty of Accession) HC Deb 20 January 1972 vol 829 cc677-809

This debate was based on both a motion to have the Treaty of Accession placed before Parliament for examination (and potential rejection) before being signed and an amendment that the Treaty would be laid before Parliament after being signed.

The motion, which would have been the more democratic and effective of the two options, was dropped in favour of the amendment which the Government was always going to have to do anyway!

This represented a disaster and a total waste of time and a missed opportunity and was merely an attempt by the pro-EEC Leader of the Opposition, Harold Wilson, to politically point score, show party unity and get the Treaty signed with the intention of trying to get better terms later, if he was then back in power. It was also the result of bad judgement on his part, due to the lack of time and the rushed nature of this process, which was frequently commented upon by Members. The Government was also able to use all of this to their advantage to evade crucial issues.

The best and most Parliamentary democratic and advantageous course of action for the Opposition, would obviously have been to use this debate to attempt to prevent the signing of the Treaty due to contempt and abuse of Parliament and the fact that Heath had the Mandate of neither Parliament nor the People and was acting Ultra Vires.

However, although not at all beneficial to the Parliamentary process at the time, this debate did bring up a number of matters of great interest to us today. This included as well as critical evidence, many facts of a practical nature that we are today unaware of such as signing the Treaty involved adopting into UK law every single rule and regulation etc. ever made by the EEC from the start well over a decade before.

This amounted to around 2,500 in number, presented in 42 large volumes in addition to this there were 10 volumes of Treaties and the Treaty of Accession itself was two volumes long and consisted of 161 terms, numerous protocols and annexes and even annexes to the annexes! Of course all of this was in addition to the enormous amount of secondary legislation, described by Mr Fred Peart as "of amazing complexity and unintelligibility" which was not even available to Parliament in English at the time of signing.

The shocking fact is that the Members did not even receive this immense quantity of documents until just a few days before the debate of 20th January after requesting them for around 12 months. Naturally, nobody then had the opportunity to even read them let alone study them, prior to the signing of the Treaty. At the Debate the Speaker criticised Members for bringing all these volumes into the Commons and blocking the gangway, but they were making a point as to the immense quantity of EEC legislation involved that the UK was having imposed on it.

What was really shocking was that Parliament had not even seen the Treaty of Accession, let alone had the opportunity to debate it prior to signature. In fact the previous general EEC debate was 28/10/71. Even more shocking, was the fact that even leading Cabinet Ministers had not seen the Treaty, a fact revealed in this debate of 20/1/72. Further, Mr Deakins stated in Parliament in this debate, that the Government were "treating the House with contempt" by not making the text of the Treaty available to the House. Mr Arthur Lewis confirmed, "We have heard it from the Minister, and we know for a fact that no member of the Government has ever seen the Treaty, let alone laid it on the Table. Is it in order for us to debate a non-existent document which no one has seen?"

Mr Fred Peart informed the House in his speech that there was an article in the Guardian under the heading 'Last minute frenzy before Treaty is signed', all about the Treaty and he stated, "If the Treaty is available to the Press and if Pressmen know its form, should it not be available to hon. Members?" He also further confirmed that much of his information had been obtained from 'Brussels leaks' and newspapers and revealed that an article in the Financial Times on the 8/1/72 had described some crucial decisions made in Brussels that had not been revealed to the House not even by the Ministers responsible for the negotiations and he commented on the fact that far more information should have been given to the House throughout the process.

He further commented that even Ministers were confused as to the severe impact of EEC regulations on matters such as agriculture. He concluded on the legal aspect of membership, "There is, therefore a great variety of complex secondary legislation which has never been debated in the House. Many of our lawyer friends will undoubtedly have a field day on this".

A small minority of Conservative MPs defied the Government, such as Mr. Anthony Fell who stated at this debate, "The Prime Minister said, in unequivocal terms which will go on being repeated ad nauseam, that he would not recommend Britain to enter the Common Market without the full-hearted support of people and Parliament. We know that, when the Prime Minister goes to sign the treaty on Saturday, he will not have won that full-hearted support. By no stretch of the imagination will the Prime Minister be able to say in truth even to himself, or perhaps only to himself, "I have the full-hearted support of the British people"".

Mr Fell then went on to say, "Not only will he be unable to say on Saturday that he has the full-hearted support of the British people, he will not even be able to say that he has the full-hearted support of the British Parliament, which he claimed to have after the vote on the 28th. Whatever majority there will be, it will not be the one-third of the majority that resulted on the 28th. How, therefore, can my right hon. Friend claim to have the full-hearted support of either the British people or the British Parliament."

He went on further to declare "..I shall be voting tonight with the people and that means voting against the Government. This may cause some mirth on the part of certain occupants of the Government Front Bench, but I assure them it is not a laughing matter when a hon. Member is forced to vote against his own Government. My opinions have been made public throughout the piece, right back to my clash with Harold Macmillan when he lit the damp squib ten years ago."

He went on to state "In my view, too strong an influence is being used on Hon. Members in advising them how to vote in Parliament. It has been going on among Conservative Hon. Members and I have no doubt it has been going on among Hon. Gentlemen opposite, but it has gone well beyond a joke."

Mr Fell went on to finish his speech with "It is in the strong light of that advice of the great Edmund Burke to his constituents that I feel free to defend my constituents' interests, and I feel that I can do that best by defending the interests of the British nation by voting against the Government on every occasion when I can do anything to support those millions of people outside this House who are avowed to support, and, have supported us in our battle against Britain going into Europe."

Mr Peter Shore stated on the subject of the high standards of Parliamentary and public approval demanded by the other applicant countries before joining the EEC, "The House will also recall that the Governments of all three applicant countries have to surmount very serious hurdles in the requirements in their constitutions of specially high Parliamentary majorities – five-sixths in the case of Denmark, and three-quarters in the case of Norway – and then follow that up in all cases by a Referendum of their people."

He then went on to further state "It is my belief that Parliament and the People of this Country are in for a profound shock when they are at last privileged to see the full text of the Treaty of Accession, for they will find, in the precise language of a carefully drafted Treaty, the reality of what was agreed during the negotiations and the commitments and obligations which this Country will have to assume." He also commented that the other applicant countries had made much better efforts to protect their own interests than the Heath Government had in the negotiations.

Those opposed to the Treaty highlighted the fact that the North Atlantic Treaty (which was much less important from a constitutional point of view) was published in the agreed text as a White Paper for Parliament 16 days before signing. In countering this the Chancellor of the Duchy of Lancaster (Geoffrey Rippon, later Lord Rippon of Hexham), who had carried out most of the negotiations, falsely claimed the Treaty of Accession was a 'draft' leading MPs to the mistaken conclusion it could be altered, later the Government confirmed it was not a draft and that he had been 'mistaken' in his opinion.

He also cited the obscure 'Ponsonby Rule' (which has now been disposed of), which was a mere constitutional 'convention' that a Treaty could be signed before Parliamentary examination. However, this could be easily dismissed as this convention pre-dated the precedent of the North Atlantic Treaty procedure and as a mere 'convention' could not apply to the Treaty of Accession, with its unique status and far reaching constitutional and political implications.

The Solicitor-General (Sir Geoffrey Howe, later Lord Howe of Aberavon), further misled the House in this debate, to believe that they could amend the Treaty of Accession during the legislative process. However, careful analysis of his words reveal all he was actually promising was mere debate and discussion.

He also falsely claimed that the Royal Prerogative alone was sufficient authority to sign the Treaty of Accession. This assumption has been discredited many times, even for minor matters, let alone regarding a Treaty of this importance. In fact Heath did not even have the mandate of his own Government and Cabinet to sign the Treaty, due to the fact that even many of his leading Ministers had not seen it, let alone the Conservative back benchers.

It is important to briefly cover Fisheries issues, as this was a recurrent issue throughout and Mr Douglas Jay stated in this debate that the Government had "falsified the main facts about the Fisheries Agreement in their official statements to Parliament". Further, Mr Jay informed the House that the Fisheries Agreement had still not been published and he considered that was a very good reason to prevent the signing of the Treaty on this basis.

There was constant criticism throughout the debate of the capitulation fisheries terms the Government had accepted, including the fact that the terms, which could never be described as favourable, were only guaranteed for 10 years until 1982, and after that it was all at the mercy of the EEC. This amounted to a far inferior deal to the one Norway had negotiated, and there was extreme anger that a permanent deal had never even being requested, with the severe impact this negligence would have on peoples' livelihoods. Similar criticism was made of the capitulation terms regarding New Zealand and the Commonwealth Sugar Agreements.

The opinion of the People was totally ignored and we discovered a very relevant fact from this debate, which represents the largest poll/ Referendum of UK voters taken at the closest time before the Treaty of Accession was signed, consisting of 6 million voters. This was revealed by Mrs Renee Short MP who stated at the Labour Party conference in the autumn of 1971 a motion opposing entry to the EEC was carried by more than 5 million votes against 1 million in favour, this confirms over 83% voted against joining the EEC, this fully reflected public opinion at the time.

Heath was in complete contempt of the public opinion and ignored his promise to the country before he was elected, when he vowed that entry to the EEC would only be with "the full-hearted support of the British People and Parliament" and his mandate to the People of the UK in his 1970 Manifesto regarding the EEC when he stated "our sole commitment is to negotiate; no more no less".

His signature on the Treaty of Accession on 22nd January 1972 was not only Ultra Vires but it was the ultimate betrayal of the British People.

The Retrospective Sham Referendum of 5th June 1975

It is the view today that the Referendum held in 1975 was the endorsement of the People for EEC/ EU membership, however this is not the case at all.

First of all, this Referendum was carried out retrospectively (after, not before, joining the EEC on 1/1/73) and there was no good reason for this being so, as there had been countless rejected requests for a Referendum in the 11 years since negotiations began in 1961. Also, thanks to the efforts of Tony Benn, legislation was in place that would have permitted a Referendum at any time over the 18 months before the UK joined the EEC on 1/1/73. In fact, a Referendum should have been held before negotiations even began, because of the massive Constitutional and Sovereignty implications.

It is also a fundamental legal concept that retrospective Legislation is not permitted, so why should a retrospective Referendum have been permitted on this basis especially with the premise always being to 'stay in'. The People should have been offered the opportunity to vote for a Party that should have automatically have just stated in the 1974 General Elections that the intention was to leave the EEC and that would be delivered upon automatically without the requirement of a further vote. It could be argued that the opportunity for a Referendum had passed, the People had not been consulted when they should have been, it was against their wishes and it was just a case of righting a wrong.

In fact legal action based upon this (as we, The People's Brexit, are currently planning) could have been enacted at any time to remove the UK from the EEC. It was always merely a case of repealing the European Communities Act 1972 which has the effect of bringing EEC/EU law into the UK. This fact was known from the start by the politicians and indeed for some was a reason that they stated they voted to support the application to join in principle in the first place, as this provided a safe guard if things went wrong.

However, in 1975 as today, the majority of Parliament (apart from a few anti-Marketeers) were determined that the UK should stay in the EEC at any cost and they used every trick and devious strategy they could think of to ensure this. Some things never change in politics, as the situation then was exactly the same as the situation now!

The retrospective Referendum of 1975 (on whether to stay in or to leave the EEC) was carried out by a very unwilling Harold Wilson, who was an ardent Pro-European, to try to satisfy the October 1974 Election Mandate he had been forced to give in order to stay in power and in an attempt to silence his Parliamentary and Party critics. He did not care about the opinion of the People as he had previously turned down Referendums on many occasions as Prime Minister before the UK joined the EEC defending these denials on the flimsy reason that it would be 'contrary to our traditions in this country' and on one of these occasions he even stated that any Ministers should resign if they took 'a contrary view'! (HC Deb 25 November 1969 vol 792 c199).

The whole 1975 Referendum was biased and reluctant from start to finish and the People were further indoctrinated and brainwashed and even bribed (with promises of cheap cigarettes and alcohol according to witnesses at the time and the Government propaganda promising great things regarding food, money and jobs) and of course there was 'project fear'. Psychologically to gain the advantage, the Referendum was devised not 'Yes' to leave and 'No' to stay in, but the reverse! Everybody knows that 'No' with all the negative associations of that word, has a distinct disadvantage from the start and 'Yes', with its positive associations has the advantage.

The 'Yes' campaign was extensively bankrolled by the EEC (this is outrageous and would be totally Illegal today!), businesses and others and all newspapers supported a 'Yes' vote apart from the left wing 'Morning Star'. Every household received a lavish booklet on 'Yes' arguments and a frugal booklet on 'No' arguments and a further booklet (at considerable Taxpayer's expense) from the Government entitled 'Britain's New Deal in Europe' stating on the front cover 'Her Majesty's Government have decided to recommend to the British people to vote for staying in the Community', Harold Wilson, Prime Minister.

This went on to be an even more biased piece of propaganda than the 'Yes' booklet with many promises of rewards and a great future with a 'Yes' vote or doom and a future of misery with a 'No' vote and resulted in every household having two 'Yes' booklets against one 'No' booklet.

It was also blatantly obvious that far more money had been poured into the 'Yes' campaign creating an Illegal bias that would be penalised with criminal charges today, in addition to much deserved condemnation of the Government.

There are also many claims that the entire Referendum was rigged (with the total vote numbers being altered in favour of staying) as it was the first National Referendum in this country and there were not the legal checks and balances that there are today so it would have been very easy to do this. This is further reaffirmed by the fact that the stakes were too high and Wilson's Minority Government could not afford to lose, so it is claimed by many that he ensured he did not.

There is no doubt at all that if he had lost the Referendum, he would have no choice but to resign as Prime Minister (as David Cameron resigned in 2016 after losing the Referendum then) also many of his Ministers would have to resign too. It was also considered that a near bankrupt UK literally could not afford a big bill that could well be demanded by EEC upon the UK leaving.

This whole argument of the malpractice of the 1975 Referendum is reinforced by the fact that legislation such as the Political Parties Elections and Referendums Act 2000 was not in force at this time, so to falsify the result would have been very easy. This is further proven by the fact that there was even an apparent need for this legislation in the first place. The legislation introduced a procedure to oversee the whole Referendum process and vote counting and to test and research proposed referendum questions, the wording of which is vitally important to avoid bias.

The exact question asked in the Referendum of 5th June 1975 was as follows:

"Do you think the United Kingdom should stay in the European Community (the Common Market)?"

This question is so biased it is outrageous, it even conveniently omits the word 'Economic' from the name of the European Economic Community to try to fool the people as to the real meaning of the EEC and the consequential importance of the decision and adds the comforting words of 'the Common Market' to further deceive the People. It is reported that much Parliamentary time was taken up in deciding upon the 'right' leading, biased question to ask.

From our research we have concluded that this Referendum was subjected to exactly the same type of oppression, deceit and manipulation as everything else concerned with the majority of the politicians of the UK and joining the EEC and the 'Yes' result should be disregarded as being a false rigged result.

The Undisputable Fact is that Under UK Constitutional Law one Parliament Cannot Bind Future Parliaments.

On behalf of the British people of today and the British people of 1961-1972 who were duped and conned by their own elected representatives and denied their say on the Sovereignty of their country, this wrong must be put right.

Some people are currently complaining about being denied their rights and wanting another Referendum, but we are only in the European Union now because the people of 1961-1972, who should have had the decision on whether or NOT to join, were denied their rights! The reason for them being denied their rights, was because the politicians knew they did NOT want to join!

UK Democracy has failed, the whole membership is illegal and we should now be using this to our advantage to get ourselves out on our own/ WTO terms and be financially compensated for it instead of paying the EU as Justice for the People of 1961-1972, many of whom fought in World War I and II, for the freedom the Politicians gave away!

Who knows what could have been achieved if they had instead built up the Commonwealth as the People would have wanted, instead of wasting a wonderful opportunity and ending up being dictated to by the 27 other European Countries, mainly Germany.

The UK is not Subject to Article 50 or any other EU oppression due to being in the EU in the first place Illegally, Unconstitutionally and Undemocratically so we need to now leave on our own/ WTO terms and be financially compensated. The EU also now owes us full co-operation to make leaving as painless as possible.

The Present and the Future

On 15th January 2019 The People's Brexit wrote to the Prime Minister and the Attorney General with our evidence of the facts that the Heath Government acted illegally and Ultra Vires between 1970 and 1974. The most notable occasion of all being when Edward Heath signed the Treaty of Accession on 22nd January 1972 without a mandate from the People or Parliament, gave away our Sovereignty and bound us to the EEC/EU.

We stated that we require the Government to acknowledge and condemn publically in Parliament that this occurred Illegally, Unconstitutionally and Undemocratically to the detriment of the British People back in 1972 and is still affecting the UK today.

We feel that we should not be hostages to history and to the actions of a small number of people, notably Edward Heath who had no right to shackle the UK to the EEC against the will of the People and the UK should not be punished further for these actions by the EU. It is the actions of these people that are causing the difficulties we are experiencing today.

Other countries have joined the EEC/EU willingly, when the People have been given a vote in a Referendum when they could choose whether to join or in the case of Norway not to join.

Unsurprisingly, we received no reply to these letters from either the Prime Minister or the Attorney General.

Another little recognised fact is that the signing of the Treaty of Accession was also Ultra Vires, due to it giving the right to tax the British People in perpetuity without their consent to a foreign power, which is against the terms of the Magna Carta and the Bill of Rights.

Prime Minister Theresa May stated in Parliament on 14th January 2019 that "the Government is a servant of the People" and now the People are demanding that the Government honours this noble statement and condemns the actions of this previous Conservative Government and takes action to resolve the situation with a new type of Brexit under our/WTO terms that includes restitution and compensation from the EU as they are at least equally and possibly more culpable for these actions.

Edward Heath could not have signed their Treaty without their co-operation and there were many secret negotiations and deals that we will never know about. To sign a nation up to a federal institution such as the EEC and take away our Sovereignty when over 83% of the people were totally against it is unforgivable and is in breach of the very foundations of the Treaty of Rome that the whole EEC was based upon.

That People could be oppressed in this way is the act of a totalitarian hierarchy, the very opposite of what former enemy occupied countries should have been trying to achieve and it is to their shame that they permitted this situation to happen.

It should have been a term of joining demanded by the EEC that the People of the UK should have been consulted by a Referendum and membership should have only be given if it was the will of the People. In addition, the joining terms given were unfair, financially costly punishment terms, that were only accepted as the politicians with the power were determined to join at all costs and this was exploited by the EEC who were only interested in how much money they could extract from the UK.

The People were further integrated into a federal Europe over the years by stealth and further Treaties, all without consideration or consultation of the People of the UK.

After years of oppression by the EEC/ EU the majority of the People of the UK who had not been brainwashed decided to vote to leave the EU in the Referendum of 2016. This result has still not been honoured and the EU still want to punish us further with unfair terms.

The People's Brexit are not prepared to accept this. It is now the responsibility of our Government to demand the justice, restitution, compensation and co-operation we are due from the EU. It is also a fact that the Treaty of Accession of 1972 is null and void (and therefore UK Membership of the EEC/EU) due to it been signed Ultra Vires, so the EU cannot hold us hostage to it or to any other Treaties signed subsequently.

Further the legislation (The European Communities Act 1972) that brought it in to UK Law is also Ultra Vires and was forced through by the abuse and contempt of Parliament by the Heath Government.

Many of our elected MPs are today still betraying the People of the UK and the Mandates of the Manifestos of their Parties, Labour and Conservative that promised Brexit in the General Election of 2017. They still want to remain in the EU, despite it also being against the will of the People in the 2016 Referendum. These MPs now need to support and deliver on these Mandates or resign their seat now. At the next General Election they will be replaced by Brexit Party MPs who will deliver the wishes of the People.

Some final important quotes from the speech of Mr Fred Peart at the Debate of 20/1/72 are, "It is a fundamental rule of our constitution that no Government must bind their successors in relation to our internal Sovereignty. The Sovereignty of Parliament does not belong to those who are at any given time its members. They hold it in trust for the People and they cannot give it up without the consent of the People."

He went on to add "We should bear in mind that there is no civilised country in the world which allows a basic constitutional change to be made without a Referendum, without the consent of the People or without a special majority of their legislatures. This is true of, for example, Denmark, Norway and Ireland. Thus, the Prime Minister will be signing the Treaty of Accession on behalf of the

British Government, but he will be ignoring Parliament and the British People."

Edward Heath did exactly this and now it is the duty of the Government on behalf of the British People to now give us justice and Brexit and take our Sovereignty back from the EU. It is also the duty of the EU to take responsibility for their role in this injustice.

It is also time in 2019 for the Government headed by a new Prime Minister to tell the truth to the People of the UK about the circumstances of our being part of the EU, it should no longer be the open secret that the people in power know about but refuse to talk about.

The majority of the public who actually thought we joined in a legal and democratic way, as they are entitled to think would and should have happened in the 20th Century in a democracy, now deserve the truth from the Government.

It is the responsibility of the Government to now deliver -

THE PEOPLE'S BREXIT

Tributes and Thanks

The People's Brexit wanted to express our tributes and thanks to the following people who have helped the cause. Firstly and very notably all the 'Anti-Marketeer' back bench MPs and Lords of all Political Parties in the 1960s and 1970s, written off as 'extremists' and 'cranks' when all they were doing was very vocally defending the Democratic Rights of the People of the UK which were being denied and oppressed in the determination to join the EEC at any cost. Reading their words desperately trying to prevent this injustice occurring they feel like old friends to us.

Secondly, all the 'Anti-Marketeers' at the time and the people who have been Anti-EEC/ EU and have been very vocal about it since. Including Vernon Colman for his useful essays on the subject, Nigel Farage and UKIP who forced the Government into having the 2016 Referendum which proved conclusively that despite over 50 years of institutional brainwashing the People still wanted to leave the EU!

Thirdly, all the People who were brave enough to stand up to the Government and vote against them and their official line to Remain and instead voted to Leave in the Referendum of 2016. This was not only a vote to Leave it was a vote for Democracy and Justice! Also, to all of the organisations that have been working hard since the Referendum towards getting the UK out of the EU, including Leave Means Leave and Get Britain Out and numerous others.

Fourthly, Nigel Farage and the Brexit Party, who came from no-where on 12th April 2019 (the second failed EU leaving date) and with a fantastic campaign for the elections for the European Parliament resulting in 29 Brexit Party MEPs who will now fight tirelessly for Brexit. Also all the rapidly increasing, signed up, supporters of The Brexit Party, keep up the good work of supporting and campaigning for the Party.

At the next General Election there will hopefully be a majority of Brexit Party MPs to replace the feckless Remainers and BRINO supporters that we currently have the misfortune of representing us.

Last but not least, the minority of Pro-Brexit Ministers and MPs of ALL Political Parties and all MPs that actually believe in a real, not fake, Brexit and Democracy. Also, not remaining in the EU Dictatorship as the majority of the current incumbents of the Parliamentary seats seem to want. Please continue to fight for the rights of the People of the UK against Oppression by the EU. Let us now tear up their unfair and unjust deal and leave on OUR OWN/WTO terms! Let us not be blackmailed into remaining in this corrupt, unjust European Union!

Theresa May's Government have failed miserably to deliver Brexit. She tried to deceive Parliament and the People by attempting to force through Parliament three times what she called the 'Withdrawal Agreement' but in fact was a Surrender Treaty, one that a country would only commit to had they been defeated in war. This Treaty was written by EU officials under the direction of Germany and benefited only the EU and punished the UK.

Her duplicity and fraud was exposed and she was forced to resign as Prime Minister. She truly was the second worse ever Prime Minister, the worse one of course being Edward Heath who illegally forced the UK into the EEC/EU in the first place, thereby nearly bankrupting the country, causing untold misery from thousands of job losses and numerous other EU caused problems and costing us a fortune over the last nearly 50 years.

It is telling that in 2019 we are only now enjoying employment rates that are the best since 1974, the year after we joined the EEC. This is still all a nightmare today from which there seems no end. Project fear is in over drive coming out with their lies and scare mongering.

We are now going to have a new Prime Minister, most likely Boris Johnson, only time will tell what type of Brexit and what type of future he can achieve for the UK in the face of a corrupt House of Commons that are attempting to defy Democracy and defy the result of the 2016 Referendum.

The UK Politicians of 1961 to date and the actions of the EEC/EU from 1961 to date have caused this problem and division, now it is the duty of the UK Politicians of 2019 to put it right and to fight for the rights of the People of the UK!

However, unfortunately, based on the failure and refusal of many past Governments to actually carry out the wishes of the People and the fact that we foresee another BRINO looming, it looks very likely that it will be up to The Brexit Party to take back our Democracy and Independence.

The Current Situation

The People's Brexit is a rapidly growing Campaign and Research Group who are determined to right the wrong and injustice that has been done and we need you and others to join our new campaign for justice for the British people of 1961-1972 (that would have included veterans of both World Wars) and ourselves.

Also, if you have not already, we need you to join us in the Brexit Party, who have 29 MEPs and now need to take control of Parliament and get rid of the current mainly Remain supporting MPs to deliver real Brexit not the fake Brexit in name only (BRINO) offered by Mrs May.

Hopefully the new PM, who is likely to be Boris Johnson, will deliver real Brexit on WTO terms. However, the Remainers may not let him and are already plotting and coming up with devious plans to prevent Brexit. Also, let us not forget that he did actually vote for the Surrender Treaty the third time so there is every likelihood that we may end up with another version of the Surrender Treaty.

Further, let us not forget that he pulled out of the Leadership Contest in 2016 and we ended up with duplicitous May for three long years by default. We suspect this was planned by the Conservative Party grandees and Johnson was rewarded with the post of Foreign Secretary. Ultimately he may end up weak and ineffective against the present determined Remain Parliament power base, at this stage we cannot speculate. However, whatever is done can be legally undone under the Constitution and particularly under the current circumstances and upon originally being forced into the EEC/EU.

The Brexit Party is not just about Brexit, we are changing the current old, broken system of politics for good. It is new politics for the 21st Century, truly democratic and where the People actually have a say in policies.

Starting by scrapping the EU dictated HS2 (saving £100 billion), reforming and greatly reducing Foreign Aid, putting money into the regions and helping small businesses, both of which the EU prevented us from doing with their regulations. Also scrapping the TV licence for the biased BBC! It is the end of the old Lib/Lab/Con that serve only themselves and not the People and the return of DEMOCRACY.

Back in 1940 'the few' heroically fought the Battle OF Britain now in 2019 it is up to us, 'the many', to heroically fight the Battle FOR Britain. We have recently commemorated the 100th anniversary of the end of the First World War so what better tribute to the fallen and those who fought in both World Wars and the Wars and Conflicts since then, to declare the UK membership of the EU Illegal and take our Sovereignty back on OUR/WTO terms not the ones that are being dictated to us by the EU.

The people of 1961-1972 that should have had a Referendum or General Election on the point of whether or not to join the Common Market were lied to, hood winked and deceived by their politicians. There is no denying that Edward Heath illegally signed the UK up to the 'Common Market' in 1972. A biased sham retrospective Referendum three years later in 1975 does not make this wrong right.

We believe that this does not end here, it does not end with the UK being forced to accept a rubbish, Undemocratic, expensive deal from the EU. The UK is in the EU illegally and the People's Brexit will be fighting in the Courts both in the UK and internationally if necessary for Brexit on UK/ WTO terms with compensation and co-operation from the EU.

The Current Brexit Legal Battle

Currently Robin Tilbrook, solicitor and Leader of the English Democrats is fighting a fantastic legal battle against the Government. This is based on the illegal actions of the Government regarding the first extension of EU membership on 29th March 2019. We have studied this case extensively and we are 100% behind it as are many other lawyers and judges.

We would encourage everybody to read about and follow and support this action in every way. Please donate to this action as it would be the end of the EU nightmare to have already have left on 29th March 2019 under WTO rules!

This case needs your support as the Remainers are out in force trying to suppress Democracy and Justice.

Details of Our Planned Legal Action

These are just some of the main legal arguments although there are many more!

LEGAL ARGUMENTS AGAINST THE GOVERNMENT

1. Probably the most important legal argument of all is that PM Edward Heath deceived the Queen into effectively signing away the Sovereignty of the United Kingdom and the British People when she gave Royal Assent to the European Communities Act 1972. Thereby breaking her sacred Coronation Oaths (including the Coronation Oath Act 1688) and vows to the People. This is an act of Treason on behalf of Heath and his Government.

2. Heath signing the Treaty of Accession to the EEC on 22/1/72 was Ultra Vires (beyond his legal powers) and against the Rule of Law as he did not have a Mandate from either the People, Parliament or even his own Government and Cabinet.

3. Joining the EEC was in breach of the Constitutional doctrine that one Parliament may not bind another Parliament.

4. Heath illegally surrendered the Sovereignty of the People by joining the EEC without their approval and against the will of over 83% of the population.

5. At the point of Heath signing the Treaty of Accession to the EEC it represented taxation without representation by a foreign power as the European Parliament was not in existence. There is also the issue of taxation by a foreign power in perpetuity without public consent which is contrary to the Bill of Rights and the Magna Carta.

6. Heath was in breach of his 1970 General Election Manifesto pledges as he only promised to only negotiate and to actually join the EEC had not been foreshadowed (stated) in it.

7. Heath illegally used the Royal Prerogative as his authority to sign the Treaty of Accession.

8. Heath's Ministers illegally used the obscure and now discredited 'Ponsonby Rule' to justify the fact that the Treaty of Accession was not laid before Parliament and published as a White Paper before signing as should have been done under the Constitutional precedent of the NATO Treaty.

9. Heath abused the whole Constitution and Parliament to create a legal loophole to circumvent the law based on the fact that this was a Treaty and there was little in the way of existing legal precedent regarding Treaties. Heath also exploited the fact that there was an Unwritten Constitution in the UK unlike most other countries.

10. Heath and the two Prime Ministers before him (Macmillan and Wilson) refused all demands for a Referendum or General Election upon entry. In fact Tony Benn had an Act in place that would permit a Referendum upon joining at any time until 1/1/73. In the end the People had no vote at all from June 1970 until the General Election of February 1974 and even then it was the same three pro-EEC main Party leaders as 1970 to choose from, stifling democracy.

11. Heath's White Paper of June 1971 (Cmnd 4715) was filled with lies, misleading and omissions on crucial issues such as the massive legal, sovereignty and constitutional implications. He and his Government illegally relied upon the 1967 White Paper on Constitutional Law produced by the Labour Government that was outdated, he crucially did not produce one of his own. He further used illegal methods to distribute a shortened version of his White Paper and the fact that he distributed it all was illegal as it had not been approved by Parliament at that stage.

12. Heath forced and won a meaningful vote on 28/11/71 by using bribery, pay roll votes, lies, misleading, threats etc. He did not include any terms about Fisheries claiming they were not concluded as he knew he would lose the vote when it was discovered how poor they were. He then falsely used his majority in this vote as the basis to commit to sign the Treaty.

13. Heath signed up a democratic county, the UK, to an undemocratic organisation, the EEC, that had links with countries that at that time were fascist.

14. Heath illegally took over the final stages of negotiations of the Labour Government and was able to use this fact to counteract arguments from the Opposition. Also capitulation terms on everything were accepted as a result of being in such a weak bargaining position. Nothing was requested in the way of special terms as other countries had received and a strict interpretation of the terms was adopted to further shackle the People. Extortionate contributions were agreed to be paid to the EEC budget which adversely affected the UK economy throughout the 1970s onwards.

15. Heath and his Ministers claimed that the Treaty was a merely a 'draft' at the time of signing when clearly it was not! They also falsely claimed that the Treaty could be altered when it in fact it could not be.

16. Most of Heath's own Ministers had not even seen the Treaty before it was signed let alone his back bench MPs or the Opposition.

17. There were 42 volumes of over 2,500 Regulations, 10 volumes of Treaties and thousands of Statutory Instruments, most of which had not even been translated let alone read, this all had to be adopted into the law as at 1/1/73. There was no mention

of this in Heath's White Paper and MPs only received the 42 volumes one week before the Treaty was signed.

18. The European Communities Act 1972 was railroaded through by Heath's abuse of Parliament. The second reading was passed by just 8 votes after the entire Government threatened to resign. The Bill was drafted in such a way that most of the over 400 amendments were declared out of Order by the Speaker. The amendments that were allowed were voted down by the Payroll, bribed, coerced and Liberals that would wait in the bar to vote. The third reading was passed by just 17 votes on 13/7/72 again after the whole Government threatened to resign and the usual bribing etc. The corrupt process was repeated in the Lords and the whole Bill passed through Parliament without a single amendment which is an almost unknown feat. It was important that no amendments were permitted as Heath did not have the time to spare in forcing through the Bill for membership for 1/1/73.

19. At no point did any of the MPs, Government or most of the Cabinet (probably just Heath and one or two of his Ministers!) see the Foreign and Commonwealth document FCO 30/1048 which was only made public in January

2002 after being kept secret under the 30 year rule. This document confirmed the loss of Sovereignty and Parliamentary freedom to legislate and concluded that it was a price worth paying and that by the time the People found out it would be too late to do anything about it as the UK would be too far integrated into the EEC!

20. When a retrospective Referendum was finally held in 1975 by a reluctant PM Harold Wilson to honour his October 1974 General Election Manifesto it was biased and rigged as he could not afford to lose it as he and probably his whole Government would have to resign and there would also probably be extensive EEC financial penalties.

21. Further EEC/EU integration was enacted by successive Governments all without consultation or permission of the People. More lies were told about the implication of these Treaties of Maastricht, Amersterdam, Nice, Lisbon and no Referendums were held unlike in other countries (but even these were repeated until the 'right' result!).

LEGAL ARGUMENTS AGAINST THE EEC/EU

1. Knowingly signing the UK up to the EEC against the will of the People of the UK was against the foundations of The Treaty of Rome 1957 and therefore the foundations of the EEC and democracy.

2. The EEC had copies of the Heath White Paper of June 1971 and were fully aware of the lies and omissions in it.

3. The EEC should have insisted upon a Referendum as a term of joining as the three other applicant countries of Denmark, Ireland and Norway all had a confirmatory Referendum in addition to the requirement of high Parliamentary majorities in favour. This should have been crucial with regard to their knowledge of the extent of UK public opposition to membership and is undemocratic in the extreme.

4. The EEC knew full well that the official position of HM Opposition was against joining the EEC.

5. The EEC had permitted an incoming Conservative Government to take over the final stages of negotiations of a previous Labour Government. Those negotiations had also previously been left open for 3 years after the veto in 1967 and they had let those continue from where they had left off.

6. The EEC inflicted punishment terms and extortion payments on the UK fuelled by the determination of Heath and Wilson before him to join the EEC at all costs.

7. It was the EECs Treaty and Heath could not have signed it if they had not permitted it.

8. Crucially other countries were not given Referendums to join the EEC, including one of founding members and the biggest financial contributor, Germany.

The Future for Brexit and How YOU Can Help to Achieve it

Now that you know more about the corruption and the injustice that the Politicians have created and how the UK was forced into the EU/EEC against the will of the People, you will probably be wanting to help finally achieve Brexit. Not the fake Brexit that May was peddling, but a real, true Brexit with EU compensation and co-operation. How can YOU help us to get the Brexit we deserve?

1. Join us in the Brexit Party and put all your efforts into helping. The current occupants of the House of Commons are mainly Remainers but they can and will be replaced at the next General Election by MPs from the Brexit Party who will carry out the wishes of the People and deliver real WTO Brexit. In addition to other democratic policies that will improve all our finances, services and future.

2. Spread the word about how the UK was forced into the EU in the first place, it is the Remainer's 'Achilles heel' and it is kept a secret! Once they know the truth it is surprising how soon they can be converted into Brexiteers.

3. Help and support Robin Tilbrook with his legal action.

4. Help and support us, The People's Brexit, with our campaign and legal action. Let us get justice and restitution at last with compensation and co-operation from the EU.

5. Do not be brainwashed by the BBC, the news programmes, newspapers and the Remain Establishment that are feeding us with a diet of Project Fear and Remain biased propaganda. Instead subscribe to our friends at Unity News Network (www.unitynewsnetwork.co.uk) who are doing great work supporting Brexit and the Union.

6. Let us not be hostages to a history of lies, manipulation and deceit by the Politicians that were supposed to represent us, the People! Be prepared to join us to fight for Brexit against the Remainers, it may prove to be a hard fight but in the words of Churchill 'We will never surrender'!

This is the Battle FOR Britain! As far as we are concerned it has just started!

Printed in Great
Britain
by Amazon